A
HUNDRED
MILLION
YEARS *of*
NECTAR
DANCES

ALSO BY RICHARD JARRETTE

Beso the Donkey

A
HUNDRED
MILLION
YEARS *of*
NECTAR
DANCES

RICHARD JARRETTE

GREEN WRITERS PRESS   *Brattleboro, Vermont*

Printed in the United States

10 9 8 7 6 5 4 3 2

Green Writers Press is a Vermont-based publisher whose
mission is to spread a message of hope and renewal through
the words and images we publish. Throughout we will adhere
to our commitment to preserving and protecting the natural
resources of the earth. To that end, a percentage of our proceeds
will be donated to the environmental activist groups like 350.
org. Green Writers Press gratefully acknowledges support from
individual donors, friends, and readers to help support the
environment and our publishing initiative.

GReen
WriTers
press

Giving Voice to Writers & Artists Who Will Make the World a Better Place
Green Writers Press | Brattleboro, Vermont
www.greenwriterspress.com

LIBRARY OF CONGRESS CONTROL NUMBER: 2015933051
ISBN: 978-0996087292

DRAWING OF BEE BY MARK RUSSELL JONES
WWW.MARKRUSSELLJONES.COM
AUTHOR PHOTO BY ELISABETH TSUBOTA
ELISABETHTSUBOTA.COM

PRINTED ON PAPER WITH PULP THAT COMES FROM FSC-CERTIFIED FORESTS, MANAGED FORESTS
THAT GUARANTEE RESPONSIBLE ENVIRONMENTAL, SOCIAL, AND ECONOMIC PRACTICES BY
LIGHTNING SOURCE ALL WOOD PRODUCT COMPONENTS USED IN BLACK & WHITE, STANDARD
COLOR, OR SELECT COLOR PAPERBACK BOOKS, UTILIZING EITHER CREAM OR WHITE BOOKBLOCK
PAPER, THEY ARE MANUFACTURED IN THE LAVERGNE, TENNESSEE PRODUCTION CENTER
ARE SUSTAINABLE FORESTRY INITIATIVE® (SFI®) CERTIFIED SOURCING

CONTENTS

II ◔ ON OUR KNEES AT THE WATER

III ⤸ SNOW GEESE

IV ⌐ A Rare Accidental

V ⌐ The Pond

for the bees

The birds and beasts all call out in sorrow,
and however senseless they seem at first,
they've reached into the depths of heaven.

—MENG CHIAO (751-814 C.E.)

PREFACE

A TASTE

My neighbor looked at the sky in wonder just before she was hurled across the veranda into a solid oak door. When revived, her first thought was that everything is up for grabs, and that's what she believes she said, over and over, seeing beyond her friends' faces—*All that we know is wrong, half-right at best, while a taste of what we don't know is bearing down on us at tremendous speed whether or not we are ready.* Amazed that she survived, we remember only her spare whisper—*The rain is on fire.*

I

THE
LARGE
MIND *of*
THE WILD

TESTIMONIUM

A man is poised to write the last line
of an eleven thousand page letter to his father
that he's been working on in prison.

He's in the habit of talking to a fly,
often found on the lip of his metal cup,
and speaks to it as he writes:

My cell has two windows onto a world that is wondrous.

To the Great Enigma

Ever since you were indistinct faces,
red and blue boats on a lampshade,

the bars of my crib, I've pondered you,
getting no closer—maybe farther away

as if my train never left the station
while the world shot by too fast.

Po Chü-i addressed his worn broom,
a winged ant, the greens of moss—

deep conversations with extraordinary
friends, praising and mourning.

I must be going the wrong way,
grappling with you gets me nowhere.

The old bench seems welcoming,
a reverent mood waited for me here.

I attend to your long sky, your hawks
heading west, your dog looking back.

Report

Beneath a ceiling of heavy clouds,
the butter lettuce seems much too green
as if the field were lit from below.
Leaves shiver, killdeer cry—

the world pours out of its house
and made us for each other
to become multilingual in anguish
until time to report back.

I wish to report that I heard the voice
of Mozart's third hand singing in a piano
which made the bright music dark,
more beautiful, earthly.

GRANDFATHER MOUNTAIN

Birch leaves yellow, walnuts fall,
the paint of moonlight lies on the fields.
White pelicans arrive towing a coastal
winter so mild conjuring death
is mostly up to you.

I climb to higher altitudes
to haunt the weather my father gave me
when I was four—

he came home alone,
left me up there on the mountain
with the wind

and with his mama,
and the daughters who never married
but had a boy a full year that time,

honeycomb for his good self,
hickory for the bad, red leaves
burning the snow.

When the moon has gone I fly on alone

I'm taken by a misreading—
When the mind has gone I fly on alone.

But it's the gone *moon*
no longer traveling with a curlew
into the night.

Still, I'm freed for a moment, working
the high air, everything
my kind.

LIVING IN PERILOUS TIMES

Six inches of the seas have lifted
into the sky and rain down.
                                    —Reuters

Late light pools on the twisty path,
woodpeckers nail evening shadows to trees
and telephone poles.

I was the baby of the family and never knew
what was going on, or why.

John Coltrane said he would ask
Thelonious Monk questions with his horn
and get answers to questions
he never thought to ask.

Last night, brother cat, the moon painted
the blossoms on our old apple tree
and the great horned owl.

Do you think this means we're going to be
alright, little cabbage white?

Unless one owl closes one eye too many
and the entire dream unravels.

We're running along the same knife edge
as the quail—are you in love with your fine
forward-curving plume, my friend?

You can walk on the sun and the moon
where they've come all this way to lie down.

Honey for the Women

Earth wins its argument again.
I sit beneath a tree to rest, filled with living
like a worm full of dirt, and I Euripides
about the women I've known.

My fingers find a crusty dead bee in the grass,
weightless, more profound than the *Song of Solomon*.
Inside its husk, a hundred million years of nectar dances,
flowers of the world, and the world's sweetness.

But I robbed the tree of a kernel of food
by picking it up and so I put it down.

If I never get up, and no one finds me,
will bees make a hive of my body as in Samson's lion
and honey, from alfalfa and sage,
next spring?

The Winter Garden

A woman loves her wintering roses,
fruit trees, crape myrtles—

every dead-looking cane stabbing
back at the frozen months.

She inspects the weapons of her people,
pronounces, *Beauty is severe.*

Her garden survives harrowing nights
squeezed into veins at the exact

center of cut-back fingers.
At a northern farm, she stops me

by the spears of a naked willow
and demands that I see it.

Halfhearted, I look through backlit
branches to the aurora borealis.

HANNAH

The black cow
grazes among yellow flowers.

Master Bankei said, *When you hear a crow caw*
beyond the temple walls
you know what it is
without thinking.

My third grade teacher said, *You'll never*
forget my name, Hannah, it's spelled
the same way backwards
and forwards.

A moment
of some enlightenment.

The cow's swishing tail and her nose
buried in the grass
spell out cow
both ways.

She also moos.

I name the cow *Hannah,*
the yellow flowers name themselves.

A WORLD GONE SNAKY

A six-foot snake in the house
tasting the air and this warm thing
in the kitchen afraid to move.

Black and white muscle glides
into the living room and I shudder.
There must be hundreds—under my bed,
coiled in the laundry basket, and shoes.

How is it possible to sleep in a world
gone snaky? Chet Baker,
too smooth, ghostly reptiles
in his veins spelling *My Funny
Valentine* with smoke.

I catch myself reading shadows
as our tongues meet inside
a kiss tasting of salt
and a nectarine.

THE THROW DOWN KINGDOM

A mature white oak throws a kingdom to my feet—
September's hot winds are part of this and hovering
    crows
extending their claws to grasp the limb.

I can make primitive mush, present the oblong
seed to the altar and praise, recall
unfettered cries of love.

Scrub jays bury more acorns in the uplands and dry
    creek beds
than usual, driven by fire and drought to preserve
their river valley—salmon-breasted

hummingbirds at the sage, forage of deer and
    woodpecker,
cabbage whites' pale green wings with the obscure
eyes, blue sky, blue feathers.

KEELED

The forest seems impatient
for night, drinks it all

along with the river
and God—

gathers the old ghosts
into black so black

it keels my mind over
exposing the encrusted hull.

In the form of Gary Snyder,
a blue-belly lizard says,

If you're afraid of snakes,
remember, they're your snakes.

THE LARGE MIND OF THE WILD

The bobcat I'm tracking from inside the house
turns and stares through tall grass
into my binoculars—rain clouds, low and dark,
press down on our seeing.

The blood orange
found by the side of the road
rests on the windowsill
like a small tired sun.

The cat disappears into a cluster of oaks
by the reservoir
and I feel drawn to return the orange
to the mud where it fell
near the horses and meadowlarks
three miles south.

Perhaps the large mind of the wild
examines our markings
employing every one
of its eyes.

COLLATERAL

White whiskers lit, and the tip of a fin there
and there—twelve spotted harbor seals

bask in the shallows of a cove near Big Sur.
Cormorants, gulls, and ducks share one rock,

all facing west. Bull kelp climbs out of its spores
toward the sun making forests, a foot

taller each day—four inches throughout
the entire coastline range for this.

THE SEA DUCK

How many killed for cotton, oil, terrible ideas?
My feelings shoot out but only so far.
Some days I sense the worms of the earth
at their work and I see leaves trembling,
feeling no greater than one worm, one leaf.
The sea duck reads the passage of the Trident
      Submarine
with its feet and makes a little quack at the stars,
bobbing above cold trenches and creatures
flashing in the sonorous deeps.

Goldfish and Palette, MATISSE, 1914

It is said to have begun as a self-portrait
after Cézanne, but Matisse
erased himself from the scene
leaving an empty balcony, some cubist
abstractions, two goldfish in a bowl, and his thumb
hooking a white palette.

I believe that his mind was flowing out over
the balcony as he disappeared
because thirty-seven million people
were about to die in a war,
close by more millions of horses and mules,
carrier pigeons, dogs,

and that the self-portrait of a great artist
in his moment
would be the fragment of a man
and two fish, one studying the tangerine
placed against the bowl
with its left eye.

The gods are what has failed to become of us

I was nobody in the wars,
a low-born peasant conscript.

For some reason I was given the chance
to speak during the siege of Troy
and groaned to my feet saying,

I yield my air to Odysseus
whose mind runs deep.
I throw my silent leaves to the stars.

The hero locked his blood-knowing eyes on me
as if inquiring which god
had taken possession of this dipshit.

When I made it home,
I buried my weapons under the pigs
and lost myself in my labors.

ETIQUETTE FOR AN EAR

My friend showed me his war trophy.

What do you say when presented
with a slice of human flesh?

Cradle it in your cupped hands,
look at the ear as long as necessary.

Pray to your mouth to say
something as valuable as silence,

to be heard by the living and the dead,

such that if the man, or woman,
could be put back together

to try again, he, or she,
would want to.

Men think they are better than grass

You died in your sleep
after a noble life.

Welcome to Paradise.

You may do whatever you want
but try not to hurt anything,
or force your will.

Breathe the four winds, sing
with the meadowlarks
and trees,

rise with the choir of grasses—

listen

how you brush the strings
of the stars.

A Ground Squirrel's Day

The mother squirrel chews rattlesnake skin and
    disguises
her pups' scent with licking.

Then she sits on a fencepost to oversee and cool her tail
which hooks down and catches the day.

It's much like the day before but everything leans a few
    hairs
farther to the north—the shadows of the trees and
    belfry.

She measures the wind with a whisker and studies sky
for raptor silhouettes against clouds gathering

for tonight's owl and moon when she'll be
    underground
with the dark splendors of worms at their feast.

PREY

The paint fell on me.

I'm afraid of horses.
They can bite off fingers or lips in a moment,
roll over the brittle cracker
of your body.

I wanted to do that to some men
who wanted to do that to me, so it is possible
that I understand horses.

Grumbling Earth broke itself apart this morning
beneath the sea sending tsunamis.
A bald eagle appears, wild pigs,
and the split-eared doe with two fawns.

Anything can happen.
We await with intense clarity.

My daughter is riding her horse—
I listen through my shoes.
Is she still there?

THE BEAUFORT SCALE

A summer's day at level #2 this moment—

You feel the wind on your face,
leaves rustle, weather vanes
begin to move.

The cabbage white has two speeds—
desperation and rest;

Lord Scrub Jay—one commandment
screeched over and over
at a gray squirrel.

Keep moving
seems to be life's rule,
easily broken—

the mouse looks astonished by death
and the valley odd

as if the smoke from each chimney
blows in one direction
a winter's morning

but from a single house
an unwavering thread rises straight up.

To Robert Aitken

Clouds seem to stand still, grow in place, edges
reaching north. I've crawled—sodden with wistful
    longings

for something absolute. I recognize the ribcage of a
    whale
in the clouds, and the crossroads I withered at in
    Greece

hitchhiking to Romania. This moment, unfurling—
honeysuckle-scented voices of children.

A View From the Bench

Beneath the canopy of an Italian Stone Pine,
in a ravine below the park, crows
gather to their council.

Hummingbirds kiss and kiss again
the autumn sage
near a bouquet of girls
making rules for their game.

Aristophanes said the Sacred Mysteries of Eleusis
are the saying of many ridiculous things,
and many serious things.

The girls consider whether
imaginary friends should have turns,
deciding—*yes*—so no one
feels bad.

The crows scatter
to the perimeter of the shade
and the world seems lucky
in every direction.

To make a prairie it takes a clover and one bee

Yesterday I was smiling like a dumb-
founded fool. Today—weepy.

No reason.

The bells of the old church
by the river, ringing—

there must be a fifth chamber,
a side door into the corner of the eye of a god.

One fertile glance—
Emily Dickinson, dark and aware,
at her window

. . . *and one bee.*

To White Yarrow

Gather fifty stalks,
set one aside.

—I Ching

Little white clouds,
I once employed a handful of your stems
to inquire of things to come.

Confucius said the Dragon of Heaven
reveals through the common,
the wise, and chance.

I was so taken by your textures and wild
perfume that I'd often forget
my question.

On the headland, white yarrow
divines white yarrow.

Hundred Percent Chance of Rain

The winter sky is dirty nickel.
Crows solve walnuts with gravity and street.
Rain will fall with the south wind.

Gut feelings roost in my rib cage—
where's that blood clot that was behind the knee?
The far-seeing condor drops her plumes
from tremendous altitude.

I have my appetites but there's hunger
from a larger place that involves me
in its hunting and gathering,

carries me up and opens the hand.

Just Joey

Churning airs raise dust and leaves
into sunlit whirlwinds
scouring the street.

Job's lord instructs his hornets.
Elijah's horses scream.

Thirty thousand single wings
come to life for the fifteen thousand
birds of my soul.

I pull down my shabby hat,
retreat a safe distance,
carry my crippled dog indoors.

A Girl Sings to Death

A girl in an orange dress climbs
the spreading cypress and sings.

She hangs like a spider monkey
and looks at things upside down.

A red-tail perched in the crown calls
to her mate on the bell tower cross.

Death has been saving an earthly
squirrel for the hawks' children.

Death has been saving a snake
for them, it has a rat in its belly.

The girl makes a place in her song
for the cries and the wind listens.

To a Gift of Rainbow Obsidian the Size of an Ear

Held to the light,
a spectral egg awakens inside
just beyond grasp

and elusive faces,
one that drowned at sea
fifty years ago with her dark eyes.

Near the hand
framing my phantoms in you,
windblown rain

drums on windowpanes
and almost reaches
my salt.

Hunger

I.

Summer's grass—the same yellow as the cat's eyes
reading me through brittle stalks.

I've never eaten a human being, but . . .

II.

Sycamore leaves fall—
strangles of mistletoe hang from the limbs.

A half-million Christmas brides, yet . . .

III.

The rain in the living—
taken by the long teeth of John D. Rockefeller.

Vanished into thin air.

To a Sacred Statue

With no one to bow,
kiss your feet, or pray to you,
what would you mean?

We'll take the birds with us
and you'll be as we once were
to your stone eyes.

Perhaps you'll join us
in the dust devils some day,
if there is day.

Rock On Highway One, JON FRANCIS

This world does not go on forever.
The edge of it is marked by a rock that is the last
tangible thing before you step into the unknown like
    a tarot fool
but without a butterfly, or a dog.

At this point, you are what emptied from your eyes
and from your chair, and your guess is as good as mine
but I'll say that you've been pushed out of your body,
    overthrown
by everything, and you are the mystery now
sharing eyes with the mystery.

Like a breeze, you might extend airy fingers
to steady yourself on the rock
before letting go and drifting over.

MY MOTHER WORRIES ABOUT MY HAT

Every spring my mother says I should buy a straw
hat so I won't overheat in summer.

I always agree but the valley's soon cold, and besides
my old Borsalino is nearly rain-proof.

She's at it again, it's August, the grapes are sugaring.
I say, *Okay,* and pluck a little spider from her hair—

hair so fine it can't hold even one of her grandmother's
tortoise shell combs.

ON THE DEATH OF GEORGES BRAQUE

Creeks in full voice after rain,
a dusting of snow on Pine Mountain.

The river unreels a thousand miles
from the finger of a willow.

Loons call, steadily reaffirming
their covenant with the horizon.

A red fox slips by attending fully,
eye to eye, without breaking stride

through winter's pared down palette,
raw sienna, burnt umber, all-embracing.

We're captured in the amber light—
the earth near, infinitely near.

II

ON
OUR
KNEES
at the
WATER

The Injured Boat

Rain last fell in April, deep
canyon ferns wither.

My skin cries out for a taste
of kind hands—

it flies off with the fantastic
birds of imagination,

my soul cleaves to the ocean
drinking the Milky Way.

A Large Kindness

I've slapped myself, I've been slapped,
to wake up understanding.

The moon came in through the window
and took my hand by the bed—

gentle as it slipped over the bull's horns
in the pasture, filled an eye of the owl

in the sycamore with a meadow
and a mouse, took my hand.

Today I'm like a child, no more than three,
a large man helping with my shoes.

The sun drifts through autumn trees
late in the oldest year of all.

GLENN GOULD SOLVES BACH

A spider joined two pines—
twenty feet apart—with a single thread.

The nerve between what I know
and what I know feels more tenuous.

Glenn Gould spread his arms wider
than the piano and played a figure

on the air, saying much of Bach
may resolve only on the keyboard

out there

This accord that's empty of all words

Hollow chimes on a breeze
in the blue oak, friends

talk into the night beneath ancient
branches—our dead climb

the stairs of undertones, vanities
keep to the shadows.

A holy hour arrives,
a starry psalter for the leaves.

WHOSE STONE IT IS

My name is on several
headstones in a family plot,

the lettering becoming
hard to read after a mere

hundred and fifty years.
It is not enough to be silent

and still, your mark will be
erased and the stone softened

around the edges, pitted,
eaten by lichens and storms,

and drawn into the earth
until there is no doubt

whose stone it is.

Formative Encounters With the Muse

The silent boy with the old eyes makes his nest
in Cats' Forest, the nighttime hideout,
and ponders television—

What does the air think about those shows
flying into the house?

They do something weird to the windows—
the house looks sick, like it ate
the blue meat.

A rat carries an egg in its mouth
from the chicken house, a voice in the radio sings,
Let me go, let me go, let me go, lover.

Grandma sends the boy into town
to sell the pig and some beans.

Put the pig money in your right shoe,
the bean money in the left, then 'pig bean
pig bean' all the way home—

lifts the hickory switch from its hooks
by the ice box, shakes it
in his face.

He drifts upward through the roof,
climbs the lightning rod, and keeps going
into the sky with the birds and clouds

from where he can see a child with a pig on a leash
walking on a dirt road through the tobacco
pulling a wagon and some beans.

On Our Knees at the Water

We covered miles of Blue Ridge lands
hunting for the spring my father
first drank from as a child.

He fought his way into a thicket of briars
at dusk and fell on his knees
at the ruined spring box—

put his head in that hole
and drank like a tired horse—*Boy,*
get on down here and drink of this water,
there is none sweeter in this world.

Somewhere in the hollows,
neither dog nor owl but the quiet,
we crawled out of our wild church
filled with the sweetness below.

In a Sunny Meadow

My father hits me so hard
my mind jumps ship.

In a sunny meadow,
I come to my senses in a body
of many voices:
mountain bluebird, meadowlark, water
singing over the rocks—

breath streaming ten thousand miles
alive with migrations and clouds—

lying on the kitchen floor
like a half-opened jackknife,
my father bending down to see
if I'm still breathing.

The dead increase their invisible honey

Nights of hard frost blacken leaves, the birch
looks more like my great-grandmother every day.
My father's down there in the valley,
by the river, with his sorrows.

All my relations and their headstones
were moved to the new cemetery
when the Interstate was cut in.

The mortician asked how closely we cared
to examine the remains.

Aunt Mildred was enthused to see
some of our dead again and said, *You know,
they don't look that bad.*

Her sister, though pruny and gray,
still looked sixteen and more certain
General Lee will rise.

I pondered my father's casket.
A steep war among his angels and demons
had always spilled over—violent, then tender,
or filled with sexual swagger.

He loved his morning glories,
birds of paradise, and a series of rabbits.
At seventeen, his father beat him one last time
and ran him off—I lit out at ten.

I was captured and whipped.
My father died at home soon after and I didn't care
for another look.

But we cracked the lid, slipped in
the photographs I'd discovered of his muscled
swains—concealed loves—and buried him
once more.

DESTINATION

Near my grandfather's birthplace in Denmark,
a mesolithic grave was discovered—

a mother's decorated body, hair splayed
on the pillow of her folded robe,
resplendent alongside the infant son
nestled close on a swan's wing
with flint blade and snail-shell beads.
Both were dusted with red ochre.

Songs and ululations—
to encourage them on their journey—
must have risen from what is now the floor
of the excavation pit I can't quite circle
because of the 20th century office building.

Sparrows, small and prolific in their wildness,
scratch and hop on the dirt mounds, flit
into the hole, and then to the crannies
and the crow-stepped gables.

To the Black Madonna

As you prepared my body
for the viewing, I was happy
and wanted my friends to meet you.

But then I was sad—
they would see only a corpse clutching
Butcherblock, the sword that drained the blood
from my king's enemies,
hand steady as a bricklayer's
building a wall,
without glory or song.

I once asked a bishop
if the Vatican harbored a secret
dogma explaining you—

it's been said that you are Isis,
or a shade of Kali.

He pondered,
you swirled in ebony on the high wall
beyond the altar of his church
near your son.

Actually, very interesting,
he said, *there is none, we just can't
get rid of her.*

I still feel the doves of your hands
and taste your lips
on the ear you whispered into
assuring me that I will
wake up.

TIMMY

I've heard last words of the dying.
My grandfather asked for the time and said, *Oh*.
Stay with me, my father pleaded, the only fear-sound
I ever heard escape his mouth. But Timmy was silent
and more vivid than the scream of a horse
painted by Pablo Picasso.

NOVEMBER 22

The news of the sky is mauve
on the belly of a horizon

cloud, the color flies eastward
and grasps the yellows

overhead, all painted on
the lucent air, all achieving

intensity of hue, as the shapes
of things blacken below

purple and Egyptian Violet
bleeding out to lavender-

grays consumed by the grief
in the bells of St. Mark's.

Sonnets to Orpheus, ii, 29,
RILKE—A VERSION

for Ekaterina
JULY 29, 1969-JULY 30, 2014

Silent friend of many distances, feel
how your breathing enlarges everything there is.
Ring out among the beams of dark steeples
into the night. Whatever feeds on you

grows mighty from your marrow.
You'll know the ways of transformation inside out.
That one grain at the core of your sorrow?
If the drink is bitter, become the wine.

Be in this night's overspilling
the mystery at the crossroads of your senses—
the magic of their strange encounter.

And if the earthly no longer speaks your name,
say to the silent earth: *I'm flowing.*
To the rushing waters add your glistening *I am.*

The cellar door used to lock with a pigtail bolt

Father, there's a good name for bread—
bread—and for wine.

All the mercy there is seems to be in the white,
late-afternoon sun of autumn—

backlit mourning doves, black as crows,
come home to their iron oak roost

with a few magpies, crows themselves
convene in the pine.

The color of the drained-of-blue sky around
the sun has no believable name,

anymore than wars do—and yet one of *them*,
backing out of my gut, is a screeching

pigtail bolt, and its pig.

An Osiris

I've been playing *rock-paper-scissors*
with Almighty God
and losing.

We go again—
do I really need this sorry skin?

Giacometti's dog, nose to the ground,
a bit of life in the tail—

the Lord says, *You are
my Nile.*

ACCOMMODATION

My mother and I have been pared down
by death, divorce, the scattering
of children and their children—

lives marked by the number of wars,
loves, and biopsies survived.

We share the silver from her second marriage,
a gift to me for my second, that travels
between my loft and her cottage
for special occasions.

We share a doctor who cuts and burns
similar oddities from our skins;

comfort rituals—
dinner together every Sunday at six
and a classic movie.

You might call this a kind of third
marriage for both of us with thoughtful
avoidance of our political views,

enjoying the silence of her garden
and the cabbage whites at their labors.

Rilke's *Spaziergang*—a version

My eyes touch the sunlit hill
far ahead of this road I've just begun—
grasped by what can't be grasped,
no matter how distant—it *is* inner light

changing me into something as I go,
almost sensing, I already am.
A gesture urges me on, in answer to mine—
I feel the wind in my face.

WATER SPRITE

Through the murky answers of darkness,
a Water Sprite kissed the underside of a world
that was basking in the pond.

I thought it was a fish, and then she arose,
naked, dripping tear-shaped pearls
engorged with light.

Dreamy, she touched me with her cattail
wand under the full Hunter's Moon
and I was the quarry.

In the morning, I knew that the solitary cloud
above the art museum in Los Angeles
last year was her.

THE TRAIL

The recluse said he
became the mountain—

western slope, peak,
no matter,

his tracks disappear
where the climb begins.

Fraying in the mist,
a thread of waterfall.

A GREAT BLUE HERON

She lifts each feather like finger,
her entire body a palette
of silent gestures.

The sky barely ripples when she plucks
a little fish from the cloud
painted on the water.

Today's Gospel

The pasture gate groans,
seven horses lift their heads—

birds in the fountain, bees
in the lavender.

SNOW
GEESE

WHITE NECTARINE

I'm leaning into my seventh decade
with my first white nectarine.

My eyes say it's an apple
but my mouth asks, *Who are you?*

Names and undulating landscapes appear
harboring wild honey.

A MARRIAGE

He began misplacing figurines
collected for a lifetime.

He liked to feel the cool
porcelain and recall the meaning
of a dog, a chicken,
ruddy duck,
but lost track of what happened
next and wept.

His wife searched pockets, odd
ledges, returned all she
could to the shelves.

To Daddy Longlegs

Without the word *delicate*,
if it stood up and walked off pages everywhere,
and we forgot about it, I could still say,
A woman gave me this little kiss
that has sixteen knees.

THE SAD TOMATOES

The tomatoes are sad,
they are sad tomatoes of poor color
due to premature and violent
separation from the vine.
Javier put them on our plates
and stares into the fire of his brick oven
with a look of despair.

A River

She's in New York, I'm in California.
Our marriage is in Missouri.

She said that our souls flow together
like underground rivers in the dark.

My heart—an old Namibian elephant
smelling water under the sand

lifting his ponderous foot to dig.
Maybe a spring down there might form

a pool, a lake, a river winding
six thousand miles.

Snow Geese

Words pale, we track
snow geese passing

in silhouette against
silver clouds—

resume talking about
how to contain

longing as the birds
disappear.

GLASS FINGERS

It is a long way to her side
of the bed. Does she also hear glass

fingers playing in the dead of winter?
The music is uncompromising—

the fingers are the cost
of the final chord.

To the Shakuhachi

Late January—
not one blossom unfuneralled.

A speechless oak upholds its empty
nest to the stars.

Do our songs cross the river with
the church bells' tolls?

Wind arrives, everything hollow
inhales the north.

I cover your dark stops and listen
for the breathing of my dead.

The rage in my belly dies on the lip
of your bees-waxed mouth.

A ghostly tongue of smoke
vanishes in the pines.

OUR JERUSALEM

The riffling around my hand
will be the ribbon of waterfall unraveling into the sea
where the canyon becomes cliff-shore.

We held each other, prayed, in the hollow
of this redwood—but its thousand years
fell across the creek in the last fire.

Our temple is now the air and its birds,
textured by fern-green shadows and long fingers
of light that let us slip away.

A Little Like Olav Hauge

We believed we could build a house for our souls,
souls miles above the Andes drawing gyres
on the air—or dark fires in the earth?

Angels of Death and Life, hundreds of feet tall,
settled on the roof when it was finished,
meaning we were terribly human.

O woman who most loves the winter garden,
cut back with precise exactitude,
because you are pleased

with the way cold moonlight drifts through the canes
and trust what you've done, trust the thin green
vein behind each thorn.

The Train

Wind swirls today's paper in a dust devil.

The sad stories put up a good fight
then lie flat in the gutter.

I've been plundered by time and left
with the usual sorrows.

Still, it takes a lot of mileage for honeyed
sunlight to overflow a peach.

She doesn't live on Chatsworth Street anymore.

While waiting on the platform,
the southbound barrels past, my reflections

in its windows like frames of a silent
movie—*Finis*.

The flower vendor asks
the sky, grumbles off with his cart,

a man counts the teeth
of an hour.

Ashes Nocturne

Three days after wildfires overswept the mountain,
we ascended from the valley
studying manzanita, oaks, pines.

All would become more prolific than ever.

We found ourselves standing in a fur
of new grass rising from ashes
near the summit

where we now entwine, and share
an orange, once every five hundred years.

FOXEN CANYON

Winds die, oceans settle, wrath
seeks distant rocks, after many years—
waves of grass, buckwheat, bees

fill their pollen baskets at the sage,
quail run in and out of the low willows
where the wild pigs sleep.

The lamb with a muddy face steps
on a length of downspout for the gutters
and makes a little bleat at her *plink*.

A flurry of bugs ignites the meadow—
flickers display bright underwings
and the bold crescents on their breasts.

The crow on the pump house
roof is overseer today and ridiculous
with a corn shuck in his beak.

A presence slips into my mouth—
like the owl returning to roost
in the skew-jawed barn—

with a language for things seen,
quiet as the stars, that hallows
woodpile and thistles.

BEGINNER

The day came when I knew nothing again,
innocent as a breeze.
I saw the shadow of a tree

slip behind a rock.
Everything laughed because everything
was in on it.

So I slipped behind a happy man
walking with his favorite dog
to the post office.

INVITATION

A swallow sleeps on a ledge of the moulding
above my door with one wing pressed
against the house.

If you're careful when stealing in
to my bed tonight,
he won't stir

but the two of us will flutter at the walls
and ceiling until the bird wakes up
from his wild dreams.

LIMINAL

The moonlit meadow is our tabernacle.
Clouds swell with light and gather.
Rabbinical owls pose their question five times.
Ocean winds loosen the trees' tongues
reading from the psalms of water.

To a Friend On His Mountain

Thank you for telling me about
last night's stars.

I'm with the evening sun and a few clouds
right now—a lot going on behind me

to the east, and there
to the west.

IV

A
RARE
ACCIDENTAL

IT'S SAID WE'RE ANGELS HAVING
A HUMAN EXPERIENCE

The hole in the day
wears a skin

with stories painted on it
like a boxcar.

The lifetime inside
breathes with its ancestors

and learned to speak
a few words.

Crows sip the oily sheen
of a puddle.

People pray to themselves
and commence killing.

Remember the lizard
licking its eyes.

It was good to find
the salty ocean,

to see a gray whale
breach and blow.

They come from remote regions of sorrow

Jesus is coming—

a crow as big as a small chicken,
acting like everything depends on him,

picks up a twig, puts it down, struts
into the crossroads and caws.

The gnarled old pear flowers—Lazarus
startles Lazarus, *I can see through my death.*

Winds plumb the hollows of a horse's skull,
the far shore near through the eyes.

THE GODOT TREE

How sad the tree was destroyed.
The tree at the Odéon was destroyed in sixty-eight.
Giacometti's tree, the Godot tree.
                                  —Samuel Beckett

Vultures flap to roosts and shut their eyes.
I brace for the wild barking and suddenly forgetful
       frogs.

The silhouette of a voice, backlit by silence,
summons me to namelessness.

Old dreams swim in the blood, coyotes
harrow Orion's dogs.

Beckett and Giacometti worked long on the Godot
       tree—
a starved tree, ridiculous, useless

for a hanging, Giacometti's dog couldn't piss on it;
a post-Death Camp tree, postmodern,

post-bees.

Heraclitus Pokes Charon In the Ribs

Leaves drift by Heraclitus who's working it out—

they say hello, he says hello, brilliant
steelhead shoot the falls.

I marry the rain snapping my hat,
it wants me,

it's irresistible,
I'm enamored as a fern.

Thirteen crows study my eyes
thirteen ways.

The river gets excited and yells,

I never step into the same
animal twice.

Heraclitus pokes Charon in the ribs
with his walking stick.

OUR CRAZY LOVE

I have decided to marry my little snake
with the moss-green skin
and obsidian eyes.

She'll glide down the aisle to the altar
where I'll be waiting
with tears of joy. A detour is possible

under the pews, after all
she is a snake. Just sit still
as she explores our side of the family.

I CONFESS TO ST. HILARY OF POITIERS

Your Excellency, I want to fill my pen
with moonlight and wild honey.

I want the goose with the letter
tied to its foot to find me.

I want the whole nectarine
and the fiery chariot, and horses.

Son, there's one problem—
the Emperor of that world is a tyrant

whose sole object
is to make a gift to the devil

of the world that Christ
suffered for.

El Gato Negro

My friend traveled to Granada to open his chest to the
    heels
of the dancers—carrying his head, with its long black

ponytail and soulful expression, on a tray—to drink
    from the source
of the deep music, to be assassinated by the moon.

My sinister lover is calling me—she revealed herself with a
    lightning bolt
singing before a thousand riderless horses in Andalusia—
her left hand on the head of a wolf.

He found a single feather in a dark corridor far inside
the Alhambra, and he wrote that its unknown

bird was fluttering against the walls of his chest for a
    long time
afterward, and that he was going to find a window.

We were to meet at a hotel by the river when he
    returned
but the door to his room was wide open—

a black cat stepped over the threshold, looked at me
without blinking, and vanished.

I think something serious happened to my friend
while he was in Granada—

I'll say that a tremor from the grave of Federico García Lorca
penetrated his shoes when the guitars bled,

and that he ran toward the knife of the Black Pharaoh
who was thirsting for him in the hidden caves of the
     cantaores.

'Show me your death, and I will show you Death,
and then you can bleed your saeta.'

That's what the Black Pharaoh said to your friend.
According to the testimony of the *Dire Wolf.*

FLEEING NEBUCHADNEZZAR

The doe with the split ear is listening
in three directions while foraging
under the oaks.

William Stafford once said to my ears,
*Maybe some things happen because
we're paying attention.*

A crow cocks one eye, then takes my picture
from the other side of his mind
and carries it off.

I climb golden Pine Mountain to greet
the dragons flying east at sunset
with their tails on fire.

Maybe if I just calm down
birds will land on my shoulders

and the one-eyed yellow cat will leap
into my arms and talk.

Mr. Evil

Last summer was cool, fall hot, winter—unseasonable.
Spring resurrected Jesus early and he is not happy.

Mother Teresa confessed, *I am Hitler in my heart,*
and almost succeeded in fighting him off.

I wanted to kill someone today, he was so cruel,
thoughtless—such inelegant tattoos.

I live behind a heavy steel door and try to remember
to set the padlock each night.

Sometimes, a bit of love song drifts through my
    window
from the beer bar at the crossroads.

SEEING

A bird shoots by my window too fast for the eyes
to follow with their clogged-with-monkeys
brain—most everything I don't know
is out there, the rest in here.

Beyond the window frame, what?
I'm startled to see four noble Italian
Cypresses after living so close by
these many years.

They sway with an evening breeze—
third from the left shorter for some reason,
say, fifty-six rather than sixty-
two feet tall;

I wonder if the neighbors would mind
if I slipped over their fence and watered that one
a bit more for a few years.
It can catch up.

I'd have to use their water and hose
of course, and they'd have to feel comfortable
seeing me through their kitchen window
during breakfast, or dinner.

Maybe they'd be kind and send out
a plate of food for the tree man, and their children
would investigate and we could make up little
games and dances, play fetch

the ball with the dog—
which I could do with one hand
while watering the tree
with the other.

It's not complicated,
unless it's Jacob my neighbors see
wrestling with the Lord
on their lawn.

St. Mary's Cathedral

My leg doesn't care about my noble thoughts.
It pressed against the leg
of the redwood table for an hour,
while I was building a cathedral for me,
and opened a door of pain two inches wide
through which vault, relics, and
pilgrims, vanished.

I think my leg would like to plant
a redwood tree and call it St. Mary's Cathedral—
an unknown species of golden brown ant
was found living hundreds of feet above the earth
among red huckleberries rooted in the trunk of
    Hyperion,
a primeval redwood surviving in a small
sanctuary near the Pacific Ocean.

I Met Our Lady of Sorrows

I was once a ferny Siberian Pea Shrub in May, delicate
yellow flowers dangling, now I'm a walker weeping.

The house we built with our many hands felt empty
with just my two, and so I became a walker weeping.

I met Our Lady of Sorrows on the road and we talked.
I was a stoic Mary, she said, *now I'm a walker weeping.*

*Lady, did your son walk on that sea like they say? Well,
it happened,* she said, *because he was the walker weeping.*

Where you came from, did you see my soul's friends?
All her fingers pointed to the ground, a walker
    weeping.

Thus the overflow of things pours into you

Pumpkins not chosen,
and their withered vines,

scattered in the field
this Thanksgiving,

to be plowed under,
expressionless—

chased by faces
ran hard

by the wolves of experience,
in time.

The cat's town mourns
the town cat, Maya,

killed by a tourist's dog
after eighteen years

working to clarify each of us.
We overflow the park

for her memorial, the ashes
ritual, the releasing,

guttering candles in hand
under the trees,

flurry of stars
through branches.

Ex Libris *Though*

On the Occasion of Nancy Gifford's *Lament*

Though wordless in many languages, prisoners leaving
    the camps
through the flues of brick chimneys into the air gave
evidence as one, and then found a field, or feather.

The soldier whose left brain was taken by shrapnel
struggles by his lake for a word he can't find
though your lips move for him.

At the bonfire of books, like a Roman Holiday,
my mind is six horses in panic, though terribly silent,
dragging the carriage in which Walt Whitman burns
    alive.

You know the bird is fluting to something
though the answer you hear from your sleepless bed
is the ringing blood in your ears.

Goddess of Mercy, Kuan-yin, though your bronze eyes
and ears appear sealed, would you be the boat gone
beyond lamentations with all of us as written?

Gate gate paragate parasangate bodhi svaha

Gone now, released one, far past returning, freed one,
    suffer no more

WINTER BIRDS OF NEW ENGLAND

Rain and sleet take turns pelting the roof
of my black umbrella on the way
to Emily Dickinson's house.

Chickadees flutter in the cut-back
Perdita roses alongside glistening slate
steps of a winter garden.

The masked cardinal in bare
honeysuckle, studying his chances
at the feeder—all heart.

Bullying jays splash seeds among
fervid nuthatches pecking their manna
from the gravel and ice.

Cupped in her hands, Emily cradles
a rare accidental that arrived
in strange weather.

FROM THE NEW TABLETS

Don't fall down the stairs.
Do not put the knife in your eye.

The commandments I need
become simpler every moment.

Lofty thoughts have plummeted down my spine
making a strangled mess
of my low back.

It appears that I've landed
as a man.

GHOSTLY VAPORS

My granddaughter fits her hand into the muddy track
of a mountain lion that prowled the graveyard
last night making dogs bark all over town.

After dinner and *Rumpelstiltskin*, the moon
illumines ghostly vapors rising from the earth
and a saltlick in the meadow like a small
lime-washed church, half-consumed.

V

THE
POND

To suffer one's death and to be reborn is not easy

The waning moon rises just
ahead of morning.

Will loss deepen all day,
regret shape the graying clouds?

Willow catkins drift, earth
listens to its lord.

⤴

Sunlight broken by leafy alders
spangles the path—burnishes

the tip of a pine needle drawn
by a one-hair brush on the sky.

⤴

What you want
may not sit with you at the table

but there is a white barn across the valley
full of many things—

iron tools, rope halter, rag, dusty
fingers of light.

⤴

Little sparrow, my breath of soul
makes brief flights and hops,
I too carry weeds in my mouth.

Emperor Hadrian hoped to enter death
with eyes open as I've seen
your brothers do.

Maybe we'll recognize the way
and meet at the threshold among those
we love for millions of days.

⤸

A snowy egret in the reeds,
utterly still, turtles in the gloom—

if that's a catfish down there,
it had more than a mile to walk

from the North Fork River.

⤸

I carried my heart hell and gone
for thrilling moments—

placed in other hands,
it grew heavier.

The old frog seems content
in his wet spot—

he blinks, and his pores go on seeing.

～

Today I am
the Gypsy knife,
tomorrow the wound,
but the knife
is also weeping
in torment.

～

The shadow of a vulture
passes through a flock of red-winged

blackbirds foraging—they rise
and settle back, their koto strummed.

～

Autumn light arrives
and a few clouds,

feathery, like the nuptial plumage
of a great white egret.

The ungraspable blue, lifting
two hawks above Grass Mountain

this evening, offers a faint
star to anyone at all.

～

It's a relief to come back from town
close the iron gate

and cross the rumbling bridge
overhung by a sycamore

that said all it could this year
before releasing the brittle tongues.

⤳

I remember the first time
the glittering little fish in a sunbeam
captured my fingers.

Today I'm taken by a flock of crows—
nine enigmas heading north
trailed by a tenth.

I glance at my hands
and discover that I've been away
for sixty years.

⤳

My words did nothing for summer
and might as well fail autumn.

The moon is on the moon
unaware of its light.

～

Leafless trees
windblown hat
no one running

～

After a long silence,
she says that Canada Geese,
flying by her wintery window,
are headed my way,
adding that we have been a near miss
for nine thousand years
because our paths always
seem to cross
without us.

～

Willows, alders, and sycamores,
follow ground-water shaping
the meadow's southern curve.

A cricket sings on a thistle stalk
below upland oaks where deer
circle onto their beds.

In the spare grass of November,
beyond the cedar and fences,
a fawn's hoof and some of its leg.

＄

Between the black clouds and stars
one loon's cry

but no sweet answer.

I call the dogs in,
hoping it's the dogs that come.

＄

Sit by the pond all day—
red squirrels become curious,
cockeyed sparrows visit.

*The entire universe will enter
your room,* Kafka said, *writhe
in ecstasy at your feet.*

But the sky—it's blue;
clouds seem to be what earth
makes of our souls,

and thirteen white pelicans,
calm, attentive, on a south wind—
the prayer flags zealous.

＄

Crows glean the fields.
I've begun to recognize individual birds

after a few years on the west-facing bench
near the chinquapin and pines.

The entire flock takes responsibility for the sickly
female that lost her neck feathers.

◡

When I give the flute a rest,
I hear the knock at my door.

My father has come to visit from death.
Was I praying?

Our fears have settled,
taken their words down below.

We stand together like tired oxen
sharing the heavy yoke.

◡

On our walk in the rainy night she asked,
Do you worship? Her disinterest

in *what*—intimidating.
In the morning, I followed the trail

of our muddy footprints through the house
and couldn't bear to erase them.

◡

A little red spider seems to be crawling
in mid-air in her hunger dance
around the blossoming sage.

Wind flows into the eyes
of a ram's skull lying in the blue
lupine and poppies.

Swallows and black phoebes
dart through *chirr* of grasshoppers
in spring meadow.

Wild pigs that rooted the oaks
last night with their gnarly snouts
sleep under the willows.

࿊

A glance is enough to sweep the Milky Way.

A few pulls on the oars
and I'm upstream before I was born.

Without ever leaving I return
empty-handed as a fish.

࿊

I forget to terminate
a vow of silence—

a whale doesn't spit me out
the third day,

no witch in the forest—
an inner eyelid

like a dog.

↪

Hannah the Cow shoos flies
around her shitty butt
with her floccus, the woolly strands
at the end of her tail.

I almost remember my tail.
I miss it—
I might hang from a limb
while reading a book;
drape it over my shoulders
in a dignified manner
like Hanuman;
manage the wine glass
and buffet plates with ease.

But if my tail once had a floccus,
I doubt that it was as fine
as Hannah's.

↪

We are quieter than the tree in the wind
and somehow agree to touch the rough bark
of its trunk at the same moment.

A liver-spotted hand, about the age
of the tree, and a three year old hand
on the gnarled Stone Pine.

↩

Late sun paints the shadow of a cloud
on the belly of the one above,

and the amber on our faces,
as deftly as taking it.

↩

Soft as alpaca, calm in my arms,
Abrazita the Donkey blinks

and extends her nose toward the sun
trying to find mother's breast.

The few white hairs on her forehead,
becoming star-shaped, remind me

to savor her magnificent error.

↩

Swallows pluck insects from the air,
hawks study the meadow from their gyres.

Downy thistle seeds take a few steps
on the pond—en pointe.

↩

The east window then the west
lit by the moon.

Darkness withdraws to a deeper place
inside the cat.

Nectar brews in the shining sage
and apple blossoms.

I drop my anchor in the silence—
it floats upward.

I can no longer distinguish prayer
from answer.

⌇

A duck, some chickens, a little toy
train, a pot of soup—some days

a cloud is a cloud and the sky,
sky blue. Night—clear heavens—

not one myth illuminated by the stars,
no decree that Abraham kill his son.

⌇

Who can be nothing
in a wind?

With fence posts and the south side
of the barn,

our moment
come.

⁓

The inkpot's dry—
emptied of lamentations
and crows.

⁓

Yet

the dulcet work
of doves

in the blossoming
palo verde—

yellow flowers
murmur.

POSTSCRIPT

MIGRANT

My soul set out, fleeing
sorrow, as a child.

Don't mourn for me,
I got a head start

to the seething heavens
in a sparrow's eye.

NOTES

Lines of other poets employed as titles, the paintings and Rilke originals, are *nectar dances* to the poems, with no certainty that I found the way.

0   The Meng Chiao epigraph is from *The Late Poems of Meng Chiao,* translated by David Hinton (Princeton, 1996).

11. *When the moon has gone I fly on alone,* from "The Curlew," W. S. Merwin, *The Shadow of Sirius* (Copper Canyon, 2008).

22. "*Goldfish and Palette,* Matisse, 1914"—Ekphrasis, Museum of Modern Art, New York.

23. *The gods are what has failed to become of us,* from "The Gods," W. S. Merwin, *The Lice* (Atheneum, 1973).

25. *Men think they are better than grass,* from "The River of Bees," W. S. Merwin, *The Lice* (Atheneum, 1973).

29. "To Robert Aitken": *I find that I don't use the word 'enlightenment' much anymore, but I do spend more time playing with small children and watching clouds.* Personal communication, Robert Aitken Roshi.

30. Aristophanes' comment on Eleusis, ("A View From the Bench") is from Roberto Calasso's *The Marriage of Cadmus and Harmony*, translated by Tim Parks (Knopf, 1993).

31. *To make a prairie it takes a clover and one bee,* from "#1779," *The Poems of Emily Dickinson—Reading Edition* (The Belknap Press of Harvard University, 2003).

39. "*Rock on Highway One,* Jon Francis"—Ekphrasis, Sullivan/Goss Gallery, Santa Barbara.

48. *This accord that's empty of all words,* from *The Mountain Poems of Hsieh Ling-yün,* translated by David Hinton (New Directions, 2001).

53. *The dead increase their invisible honey,* from "Provision," W.S. Merwin, *The Lice* (Atheneum, 1973).

60. *The cellar door used to lock with a pigtail bolt,* from "The Door," Jean Follain, *W.S. Merwin Selected Translations* (Copper Canyon, 2013).

61. *Giacometti's dog. . .*("An Osiris" and page 93 "The Godot Tree")—Alberto Giacometti's sculpture, *Le Chien,* 1951," *. . . an astonishing, tragic self-portrait."*—Charles Juliet in *Giacometti* (Universe Books, 1986).

92. *They come from remote regions of sorrow,* from "The Poem of the Saeta," translated by Lysander Kemp, *The Selected Poems of Federico García Lorca* (New

Directions, 1955). *I can see through my death,* from
The Selected Poems of Tu Fu, translated by David
Hinton (New Directions, 1988).

104. *walker weeping* . . . ("I Met Our Lady of
Sorrows")—Walker Weeping Caragana, *caragana
arborescens,* Siberian Pea Shrub. Artist and publisher
(*Sleet Magazine*), Susan Solomon, planted one
and knew that I would appreciate an encounter
with its names. Its tendrils grow toward the ground
like a weeping willow.

105. *Thus the overflow of things pours into you,* from *The
Book of Hours: Love Poems to God, ii, 10,* Rainer
Maria Rilke, translated by Anita Barrow and Joanna
Macy (Riverhead Books, 1996).

113. *To suffer one's death and to be reborn is not easy,*
from a poster of the sixties—Fritz Perls' photo and
quote on his *Gestalt Therapy Verbatim* (Real People
Press, 1969).

114. *Little sparrow* . . . ("The Pond") is after a poem
attributed to Hadrian and a few words on his
tomb as cited by Marguerite Yourcenar in *Memoirs
of Hadrian* (Modern Library, 1984).

118. *The entire universe* . . . ("The Pond") is adapted
from *The Zürau Aphorisms of Franz Kafka,*
translated by Michael Hofmann, Commentary by
Roberto Calasso (Schocken, 2006).

ACKNOWLEDGEMENTS

I am grateful to the publications in which the following poems first appeared, sometimes in different versions.

Broadsider (Paul Fericano, Publisher), "A View from the Bench"

Connotations, "A Taste," "Hannah," "Testimonium"

Green Writers Press Zine, Fall, 2014, "Formative Encounters With The Muse," "Honey For the Women"

Mas Tequila Review, "*The gods are what has failed to become of us,*" "Our Crazy Love"

Red Bird Chapbooks, Broadside Project, July, 2103, "The Large Mind of the Wild"

Sleet Magazine, Spring, 2012, *When the moon has gone I fly on alone* (Pushcart nominee as "A Possible Survivor"), "Report," "Timmy"

Sleet Magazine, Summer, 2013, "The Pond" (Sections 1-9).

Sleet Magazine, Fall, 2013, "On the Death of Georges Braque," "To the Great Enigma," "*They come from remote regions of sorrow,*" "Just Joey," "To a Gift of Rainbow Obsidian the Size of an Ear," "Hundred Percent Chance of Rain," "Fleeing Nubuchadnezzar," "Today's Gospel"

The Tree Museum, "The Godot Tree" for *SWARM,*
   A Collaboration With Bees— "chasing daphne" by
   Penelope Stewart

Water-Stone Review #14, "Goldfish and Palette, Matisse,
   1914," "Living In Perilous Times"

Water-Stone Review #15, "The Sea Duck" (Jane Kenyon
   Prize Finalist)

My thanks to Dan Gerber for reading and advising me
on some of these poems and previously for *Beso the
Donkey.*

Many thanks for comment and encouragement to
Larry Miller, Gerald Dipego, Gretchen Marquette, Susan
Solomon, W. S. Merwin, Jane Hirshfield, Joe Stroud,
David Ferry, Marsha Truman Cooper, Sam Hamill, David
Hinton, Yun Wang, Caleb Beissert, Nancy Gifford, Ellen
Doré Watson, Josh Gaines, Daniel McNeet, Kristine Jones
Brouillet, Sterling Price, Ron Colone, Barry Spacks,
Marlea F. Jarrette, Luca Crestanelli, Beatrice Hallig, Paul
Fericano, Elaine Nakashima, Perie Longo, Kristi Hundt,
Tim Elwell, Mark Russell Jones, Cynthia Carbone Ward,
Denise Cabral Yanez, and to Ruth Anderson Jarrette.

All of you variously inspired these poems, and they are
dedicated to each of you with affection and gratitude,
and to Gary Snyder for the groundwork. Thank you
Dede Cummings and everyone at Green Writers Press
for your skill, humanity, and heart, in this book and in
our world.

A NOTE ON THE TYPE

A Hundred Million Years of Nectar Dances was typset in Bembo. Bembo was modeled on typefaces cut by Francesco Griffo for Aldus Manutius' printing of *De Aetna* in 1495 in Venice, a book by classicist Pietro Bembo about his visit to Mount Etna. The Bembo typeface was cut by Francesco Griffo, a Venetian goldsmith who had become a punchcutter and worked for revered printer Aldus Manutius. Griffo's design is considered one of the first of the old style typefaces, which include Garamond, that were used as staple text types in Europe for 200 years. Stanley Morison supervised the design of Bembo for the Monotype Corporation in 1929. Bembo is a fine text face because of its well-proportioned letterforms, functional serifs, and lack of peculiarities; the italic is modeled on the handwriting of the Renaissance scribe Giovanni Tagliente. Books and other texts set in Bembo can encompass a large variety of subjects and formats because of its quiet classical beauty and its high readability.

DESIGNED BY DEDE CUMMINGS

WEST BRATTLEBORO, VERMONT